Let These Words

Relax Your Mind

~Seven Steps to a Relaxed Mind~

From the Heart of

Elizabeth Jenkins Caspian, MD

Disclaimer: This is an inspirational book intended to speak more to your heart than to your intellect. This book is not offered as a medical opinion based on scientific facts; the content is strictly the heart-felt opinions of the author. This book does not make any claim to diagnose, treat, nor cure any mental/physical disorder. If you are suffering from mental stress and strain, you are encouraged to seek professional advice and assistance.

Published and Distributed by:
Center for Creative Change, LLC
2380 N. Oakmont Drive
Flagstaff, AZ 86004

http://relaxyourmind.org

All rights reserved. No part of this book may be reproduced in any form, except for brief excerpts for the purpose of review, without written permission from the publisher.

ISBN: 978-0-692-01308-3
Copyright 2011
Center for Creative Change, LLC
Printed by 48-Hour Books

DEDICATION

These words are dedicated to the healing power of LOVE.

I joyfully acknowledge my husband,
Barry C. George.
Your love has brightened my life;
your faith in me gives me strength.
I am truly blessed to share my life with you.
Thank you for supporting this writing
project. Who knew what an adventure
this project would be?

ACKNOWLEDGMENTS

Mom, Dad, Teresa, Betty, Joel, Walter, Alana, "Sisters of the Heart", and Donna– your support is deeply appreciated, and I wish to say thank you!

Alan Cohen–your mentorship and your books are a blessing, and I am sincerely grateful.

Gerald Jampolsky, M. D. –thank you for your inspirational books, I appreciate your wisdom.

Phish, Xavier Rudd, Mishka, and Railroad Earth— thank you for the music that feeds my soul and keeps my heart joyful.

Sara, Sherri, and Mark (aka Eagle Eye) – thank you for your editing assistance, your input was invaluable.

CONTENTS

Author's Note........................... 9

Introduction........................... 13

Seven Steps to a Relaxed Mind

Step One............................30

   Safety, Security and Gratitude

     "Messenger of Truth, Viktor Frankl"

Step Two............................40

   Creativity and Possibility

     "Be the Elephant at the Watering Hole of Life"

Step Three..........................50

   Inner Wisdom and Highest Truth

     "Mr. Piper Learns to Allow His Soul to Drive"

Step Four........................... 62

Express Love and Experience

Inner Peace

"The Love of a Dog Heals the Heart and Soul"

Step Five........................... 74

Speak of Love

"Words Serve a Greater Good"

Step Six........................... 86

Think Loving Creative Thoughts

"Thoughts of Love Will See You Through"

Step Seven........................... 98

Appreciate the Source, All is One

"Looking into Infinity"

Afterword..........................111
> Meditation for a Relaxed Mind

Appendix:..........................119
> The Biopsychosocial Model
> Suggested Healthy Brain Habits

Endnotes..........................128

AUTHOR'S NOTE

"What I have could be a message,
or just some words from my heart."

-Xavier Rudd

As a psychiatrist, I provide care to people who are feeling overwhelmed by challenges. Over the years, I have gained a deep spiritual knowing that every person has within themselves a courageous human spirit that is able to overcome adversity with dignity and grace. I know we all have the capacity to stand atop a mountain of wisdom gained by facing our challenges, and learning valuable lessons from these life experiences.

I am honored to work with clients who are willing to acknowledge that they have temporarily "lost their relaxed minds." They bravely reach for support, while working to restore their inner peace. They make a healthy choice to move beyond a life of chaos, mental confusion, and emotional pain.

I encourage you to reach out for assistance when you feel overwhelmed by sadness, loneliness, and fear: at times we all need, and deserve support. When needed, work with a healing professional that can maintain awareness of miraculous solutions awaiting your discovery.

I have gained steadfast faith in the Source of life and the unseen solutions that await each client beyond their challenges. Clients, who are willing to allow for inner growth, will find themselves stronger and more fulfilled than before their challenges. <u>Solutions are always waiting to be discovered. This is the miracle of life.</u> What an honor for me to witness "everyday miracles" of mental, physical, and spiritual growth.

I share these words from my heart. I do hope this book inspires you to <u>love more and fear less</u>, as you make healthy choices that allow you to relax your mind. It has been said to teach what you most want to know; I most want to know how to relax my mind in a sometimes challenging and fast-paced world. I know for certain that a relaxed mind is much too valuable to lose!

It is important to realize we are never stuck in a negative situation; there are infinite possibilities for self-expression in life. When we relax our minds, foster a life-affirming attitude, and create a better life for ourselves; we give others hope that they can do the same. We all have the opportunity to support one another and to make a difference in each other's lives. Your willingness to be kind and compassionate to yourself and to others makes the whole world a gentler place to inhabit. I want you to know that your choices in life matter, as you are part of the web of life. The truth is- humanity is in need of your more loving, less fearful, relaxed mind.

Elizabeth Jenkins Caspian, MD
January 2011, Flagstaff, AZ

INTRODUCTION

"Become a possibilitarian.
No matter how dark things seem to be,
or actually are, raise your sights
and see possibilities—
always see them,
for they're always there."

—Norman Vincent Peale

The Power of the Human Spirit

At times, we all struggle with a tense, overwhelmed mind. When challenged by difficult life situations we feel as though our inner peace will never be restored. Yet, we have a choice:

➢ to linger in our pain and misery– and become a victim of a difficult life story.

➢ or, to develop inner strength and wisdom from the challenge, restoring inner peace without delay– and become a wise example to others.

I have worked with many people who have lost children, felt betrayed by a family member or friend, faced cancer, survived child abuse, and numerous other challenges. I have personally witnessed the power of the human spirit to rise above adversity. I know we all have remarkable emotional strength and inner wisdom to guide us back to our inner peace.

Many Paths to the Same Place

How do we rise above our challenges? In my experience we rise above our challenges when we commit to establishing inner peace, regardless of external circumstances. With courage, we seek out supportive mental, physical, and spiritual healing modalities. We discover there are many paths that lead to the same place— a restored state of inner peace, resulting in a relaxed state of mind.

The Best Solutions Come from a Relaxed Mind

When confronted with challenges we all tend to experience fearful thoughts. Yet, it is important to recognize that fearful thoughts deplete us of energy and leave us feeling doubtful, tense, and imbalanced. The best solutions come from an energized, confident, and relaxed mind. Thus, fearful thoughts do not typically serve us well.

When we catch our mind dwelling on thoughts of fear, we can choose to be aware of those thoughts. With awareness, we can elect to redirect our mind toward loving thoughts of gratitude, peace, and harmony. In this balanced state, we will discover the best solutions to our challenges.

Seek a Gentle Guide

If you find yourself struggling with intense emotional pain or mental confusion about important issues, and your mind feels stuck on thoughts of fear, it is truly wise to seek assistance from a compassionate professional. Give yourself permission to seek support, as you restore your inner peace and balance.

Living in Balance

One of the primary reasons we get stuck on thoughts of fear is that we fail to notice when we are living out of balance. For example, when we listen to fear based media broadcasts more than we listen to inspirational broadcasts, we expend more energy in a fearful state than we generate in an inspired state. Thus, we are left feeling imbalanced and tense: we lose our relaxed minds. When we generate energy and expend energy in a more harmonious way, we feel more at ease in our lives, and we retain our relaxed minds.

Pay attention to all the areas of your life that leave you feeling energized, as opposed to those areas that leave you feeling depleted. Are you choosing to live in balance? Recognize the importance of activities that restore you to a balanced state. Choose to make living in balance a priority!

Be Proactive

You deserve a comprehensive approach to restoring your emotional stability and mental clarity. A relaxed mind is the result of attending to your biological, psychological, and social needs (see appendix, The Biopsychosocial Model). If only a relaxed mind were as simple as a remedy, a vitamin, or a prescribed medication. The mind is simply too complex for a one-time, rapid-acting solution for maintaining balance and inner peace. Lasting solutions are multi-faceted, requiring our full participation as we reestablish a relaxed state of mind.

The "Seven Story Mountain"

"It's a seven story mountain...going to find a light and fill my heart again..."

- Todd Shaeffer/Railroad Earth

The quest for inner peace is an active process. With daily practice you can balance your mind, body, and spirit. You can live a life with greater meaning and purpose as you master maintaining inner peace. You deserve a harmonious life. A relaxed mind is worth all the effort you give to maintaining a balanced way of life.

When you are presented with challenges, it is important to "find a light and fill your heart again." Challenges can be rewarding, like climbing a mountain. When you arrive at the solution beyond the challenge your heart is full once more, like the climber who views the breath-taking, expansive landscape from atop the mountain. You can envision ever-expanding potential for your life beyond adversity.

The seven steps presented in this book can assist you in rising above seven basic challenges that we face in life as follows:

- Feeling unsafe or threatened in some way
- Dwelling upon negative, limiting thoughts about yourself and life situations
- Feeling lost and without a clear direction
- Feeling as though you are not lovable and the world is unkind

- Dwelling on words that have been spoken to you, or by you, in a hurtful manner
- Thinking more about your problems than you think about the solutions to your problems
- Feeling as though it is "you against the world", as though you are disconnected from the Source of life

Recognize that each of these challenges can be overcome if you climb this "seven story mountain" and view your life from a higher, life-affirming, solution-focused perspective. When you realize the power of your "Spiritual self" to guide your mind to higher ground, your life becomes an adventurous journey. Your mind and body benefit when you choose to view challenges as opportunities to climb to higher levels of awareness. Celebrate the wisdom and inner strength gained when your challenges are courageously overcome!

Seven Steps to a Relaxed Mind

This book suggests seven psychological steps that support a relaxed state of mind. Utilize these steps as part of a comprehensive approach to relaxing your mind and rediscovering inner peace. Keep in mind that this is one of many healing approaches: seek out the approach that works best for you.

These seven steps are based on ancient observations of the human biophysical energy system— the chakra system. This system can be simplified with the following obvious, but profound statements:

➤ Positive emotional energy generates positive life experiences.

➤ Negative emotional energy generates negative life experiences.

As you direct your focus inward and increase awareness of your internal energy dynamics, you are better able to restore your mind, body, and spirit to a balanced and peaceful state.

"Tension is who you think you should be.

Relaxation is who you are."

—Chinese Proverb

Let These Words Relax Your Mind

This book is offered as one of many paths to inner peace. As you read, take to heart what works for you and leave what does not work. You are wise; you know when recommendations feel helpful and when they do not feel helpful.

The intention of this book is to assist you in releasing any negative or fearful thoughts that have guided you away from inner peace. I suggest seven steps to relax your mind, and restore a sense of empowerment and calmness within. Each step begins with an affirmation, followed by a suggested prayer/meditation. As you inhale and exhale, contemplate the meaning of that step.

A brief discussion is followed by a short, illustrative story. The stories are meant to convey the energetic message of each step. Allow your mind to relax as you read: allow your heart to guide the way.

Each step ends with questions for self reflection. Blank space was made available for you to record any heart-felt ideas you might have experienced as you contemplated each step. Listen to your heart speak as you reflect on these questions, and learn to maintain your relaxed state of mind one step at a time.

Seven Steps To Relax Your Mind

Relax Your Mind
Step One

Acknowledge that you are
safe and secure.

Your needs have been graciously met
by a Source greater than yourself.

Feel grateful for the miracle of life.

Dwell on thoughts of gratitude and
redirect your mind away from
limiting, fearful thoughts.

Inhale:

I am safe and secure. I am grateful to the Source of life for all that I have.

Exhale:

I release any negative, fearful thoughts that distract me from feeling grateful for another day of life.

At times, we all lose sight of what is going well in our lives. We forget that life is truly majestic. Life made possible by the air we breathe, the soil in which plants grow, the rain that feeds the plants, and the radiant energy of the sun. Life is a miracle. The very air you breathe is a gift from the Source of all life.

We have a choice:

> (1) to dwell on the miracle of life and fill our minds with thoughts of gratitude, or
>
> (2) to dwell on the difficulties of life and fill our minds with thoughts of fear and suffering.

When we shift our thoughts to what is good about our lives we feel grateful, strong, and empowered. The simple truth - what we choose to dwell upon becomes the reality of our lives.

Any guess as to the choice the news media would guide you to dwell upon? In a media driven, politically divisive world it is more important than ever to reclaim your relaxed mind, as you are bombarded with fear-driven messages every day. Together, we can spread much needed love and gratitude in our communities if we choose to dwell on the miracle of life and reclaim our grateful, relaxed minds.

Redirect your fearful mind to thoughts of strength that rise up from a grateful heart. Share thoughts of gratitude with your family, friends, and neighbors. Dwell upon the goodness of life and feel your mind relax.

Messenger of Truth, Viktor Frankl

Your tense mind might be thinking, "These ideas seem unrealistic and overly optimistic. Obviously, this writer does not experience fears similar to mine. I have a right to feel afraid." Of course you do. You also have the right to feel peaceful and secure! Your choice, fear or peace, will make all the difference in your life.

One of the most profound messages of hope and love in the face of extreme despair comes from Viktor Frankl's *Man's Search for Meaning*. While imprisoned in a concentration camp, Dr. Frankl chose to reclaim his mind from his captors by "deepening his spiritual life". Even as a prisoner, Frankl chose to experience deep appreciation for a beautiful sunrise. He chose to dwell upon his love for his wife. He gave us a remarkable example of the capacity of the human spirit to rise above even the most desperate of circumstances.

Frankl states, "It is possible to practice the art of living even in a concentration camp....a very trifling thing can cause the greatest of joys." He gives an example of finding pleasure in having a cook treat men equally when ladling the soup. " We were grateful for the smallest of mercies...He was the only cook...who dealt out the soup equally...(he) did not make favorites of his personal friends or countrymen, picking out potatoes for them; while others got watery soup skimmed from the top."[1]

Frankl writes so beautifully of the power he and fellow prisoners gained by "retreat(ing) from their terrible surroundings to a life of inner riches and spiritual freedom".[2] While reading this book, you realize how mentally healthy it is to develop a sound spiritual life. The inspiring words of Frankl remind us of the human capacity to turn away from despair and to go within to that rich and free space created by a loving, grateful spirit.

Frankl did not allow his mind to dwell on his desperate circumstances. He surrendered his fearful mind to his powerful spirit. He writes, "I sensed my spirit piercing the enveloping gloom. I felt it transcend that hopeless, meaningless world".³

Know that regardless of your situation, you can find inner peace if you choose to put your spirit in charge of your mind: Viktor Frankl was a profound messenger of this truth. He reminds us that when your spirit directs your mind, you can allow yourself to feel safe and secure internally, regardless of external physical conditions beyond your control. Let spirit direct your life and you will feel your mind relax.

"Forces beyond your control can take away everything you possess except one thing, your freedom to choose how you will respond to the situation...you can always control what you feel and do about what happens to you."
—Harold Kushner

Relax Your Mind
Mental Exercise

How would you complete the following sentences?

I am grateful for _____.

Regardless of ____ (this situation) ___, I am free to choose my attitude and my reactions to the situation.

I can release my fears about_____.

When you notice your mind directing you to dwell upon fearful thoughts, think of Viktor Frankl. Remind yourself that you can choose inner peace regardless of your circumstances. Frankl's life was an example of this profound truth. May we all learn to rely on our spirit more and our limiting fearful thoughts less, no matter what our external circumstances may be.

Reflections:

"It is this spiritual freedom—
which cannot be taken away—
that makes life meaningful
and purposeful."

—Viktor Frankl

Relax Your Mind
Step Two

Recall that you are a creative being.

There are unlimited possibilities
for expressing your unique,
creative energy in this life.

Move beyond your fear-based mind.

Create the satisfying life
you are here to live.
You deserve a fulfilling life!

Inhale:
I am creative and unique; there
are infinite possibilities for my life.

Exhale:
I release critical, limiting thoughts
about myself and life.

While growing up, many of us absorbed negative, limiting thoughts about ourselves and life from some negative people and/or events in our lives. Is it any wonder why our creative minds became tense and unsettled by these negative influences? Rather than question these critical assessments, we took them to heart as if they were the truth. As an adult the authentic truth about you is yours to decide.

Are you willing to examine your thoughts, and take issue with beliefs that limit you in some way? Are you ready to see yourself as the new author of your life story from this day forward? Only when you choose to see yourself as an innocent child, before you identified with any negative criticism, can you freely express your unique creative energy to the fullest capacity.

Believe you are full of child-like creative energy as you decide to take your mind beyond negative, critical thinking. Hear the laughter of a happy child and feel the joy. Remember who you were before you allowed others to determine your self-worth. One day at a time, starting today, create a new life story with tales of joy and wonder, and feel your mind relax.

<u>Be the Elephant at the Watering Hole of Life!</u>

Imagine yourself in Africa, observing animals at a watering hole overflowing from the seasonal rains. Notice the animals cautiously approaching the life giving water. The zebras approach with great caution, unsure if an aggressive lion will attack. The gazelles lower their heads ever so slowly, fearing a gator will rise up and strike as they drink.

Along come the elephants. These amazing animals are massive and peaceful, commanding respect without being aggressive. Gently, they suck water with their long trunks and slowly meander away from the watering hole.

In life, we are given a choice of roles to play. Some choose to be the lions, eager to attack. Others play the role of timid zebras and gazelles, moving in life with extreme caution and fear. Some are the sneaky, snappy gators, keeping us all off guard and uncertain.

When you choose to write a creative life story, you become like the elephant. Your mental and emotional energy expand: you move peacefully and gracefully in life. You become great in Spirit!

Like the animals needing water to survive, we all need to feel safe, secure, and creative to stay emotionally vital and alive. If we believe in our child-like creative energy, rather than our critical thoughts, we no longer need to play it safe and small. We feel ourselves moving through our lives like a giant, graceful elephant.

Your belief in the creative and innocent child within, allows your mind to relax and expand. You no longer identify with limiting, critical messages from your past. Like a massive elephant, you discover a life-affirming, creative, "large self" within your being. You become free to let the world experience your authentic, creative self: you no longer allow fear of criticism to rule your mind. Ahhh, the sweetness of an expanded, "elephant-sized", self-assured, and relaxed mind!

"All limits exist only in thought,

and that is where they are overcome."

— Alan Cohen

Relax Your Mind
Mental Exercise

How would you complete the following sentences?

I choose to release the following critical, negative thoughts from my past: _____.

My creative, expansive spirit is calling me to

_____.

You have an abundant supply of creative energy to share with the world. Move beyond any negative self-talk; quiet your inner critic. Release all judgmental opinions that you hold about yourself, or that you perceive others hold of you. Let your unique, creative energy flow from within. The world is much brighter when individuals allow their inner light to shine forth for all to enjoy.

Reflections:

"Whether you think you can
or think you can't -
you are right."

— Henry Ford

Relax Your Mind
Step Three

You were born with an inner knowing of what is right and true for you.

Trust your "heart's wisdom" and your "gut reactions".

Quiet your mind and feel your inner wisdom directing you to your highest truth.

Inhale:

I listen for inner wisdom and trust my inner guidance to direct me.

Exhale:

I release doubt and

mental confusion.

As a human being, you have a large, dominant frontal lobe in your brain. This busy, thought-generating machine rarely takes a rest; labeling, comparing, judging, wanting, critiquing, planning...on and on goes this remarkable thinking machine.

Your brain is supported by many organ systems contained in a very impressive "body-mobile". The billions of coordinated functions that make your life possible is mind boggling. Your brain, supported by your body-mobile, is a highly orchestrated miracle.

You are wise to pause and contemplate this question: who is driving your body-mobile? Who is steering your life? Are you in tune with your inner wisdom and your highest truth?

Does your "thinking brain" really make the best driver in your life? In my experience, No! The thinking brain gathers information, makes comparisons and directs your actions. It is a wonderful task master, constantly grading your performance in life. However, it does not take your heart's wisdom very seriously.

Your most fulfilling life is attained by balancing the thinking mind with your inner wisdom. Learn to quiet your mind, listen to your calm inner voice, and you will arrive at your most satisfying destinations in life. You deserve to experience the joy of a balanced life.

Mr. Piper Learns to Allow His Soul to Drive

Mr. Piper sensed his thinking mind was driving him crazy. His mind was always on and never made time for inner peace. Constant thoughts– all day, every day: "You are too fat...your daughter is too thin. Your car is too old...the neighbor's car is much nicer...How does he get all that vacation time...Why is your work life more demanding than his...Look how relaxed he seems...Why are you so stressed out?"

Driving to work early one morning, Mr. Piper tuned his radio to a talk show. He heard a life-coach encouraging listeners: "Don't let your "thinking brain" wreck your life. Your thinking mind will drive you crazy with thoughts of how "too much" or "not enough" you are."

The coach continued, "Why don't you let your soul drive you away from an unsettled mind toward a peaceful mind? Hand the steering wheel of your life over to your soul. Ask your busy mind to occupy the passenger seat. Allow your mind to be a more relaxed companion to your soul, and enjoy a more gratifying life journey."

This coach seemed to be speaking directly to him. His thinking mind immediately took the wheel; "Let your soul drive? Ha! You don't even believe in a soul. Let it drive? How ridiculous! Turn this nonsense off before you really lose your mind." Yet, something inside him could not turn the station.

The life coach continued, "For those of you saying to yourself that you don't buy into the word soul, let me speak to you for a minute. Think of your soul as your higher-self: it is the part of you that is activated when you pet a puppy, enjoy a great song, or marvel at a spectacular sunset. Your soul is the part of you that has a greater perspective on life than your busy, critical thinking mind. Your soul is that part of your inner being seeking peace beyond your speeding mind."

Mr. Piper looked at his odometer. Sure enough he was speeding at 80 mph in a 55 mph zone! "Is this guy reading my mind?" he thought to himself as he slowed down his vehicle. He continued to listen as the life-coach reviewed the many health benefits of a more relaxed and soulful state of mind. "Your body-mobile will require fewer repairs. Your immune system will function at a higher level more of the time. Your heart rhythm will be more balanced and you will feel more vigor and enjoy more vitality."

Mr. Piper thought to himself, "vigor, vitality, healthier, more relaxed...tell me more!" His thinking mind was unrelenting, "peaceful people are not successful, this coach is clueless...turn this off, you are too smart for such nonsense." Yet, he did not turn the station.

It occurred to him that he must have put his thinking mind in the passenger seat. He could sense his soul guiding him as he made his way to the office. He knew it was no coincidence that he tuned in to this show. He heard words he had been longing to hear: "There is a better way; you deserve a more relaxed way of life!"

As the show ended the coach gave an invitation: "If you felt your soul longing for more, call me for a private session. Your soul is begging to steer you to the most satisfying, healthy, and loving places in life. Your soul will make friends with your thinking mind and be gentle with your body-mobile. You will discover a world of peace when you turn the steering wheel of life over to your soul."

Mr. Piper felt the shift. His soul reached for his cell phone. "Hello, this is Mr. Piper. I would like to schedule a private session. My mind is ready for a more relaxed way of life!" he heard his soul joyfully proclaim.

"All men should strive to learn before they die what they are running from, and to, and why."

—James Thurber

Relax Your Mind
Mental Exercise

How would you complete the following sentences?

My mind is most quiet and I can hear my heart speak when I _____.

I hear my heart and soul encouraging me to

_____.

In this fast paced, information overloaded world, it is more important than ever to quiet your mind and experience inner peace. Realize that success without happiness and heart-felt satisfaction is not success at all. Wise people balance their directive mind with the creative wisdom of their heart and soul. Wise people create balanced, peaceful lives.

Give yourself quiet time each day. Spend time in nature. Pray and meditate, while breathing deeply and slowly. Tune into your inner wisdom throughout your day. You, and all those with whom you come in contact, will greatly benefit from your relaxed mind.

Reflections:

"We're here to find that dimension within ourselves that is deeper than thought."

—Eckhart Tolle

Relax Your Mind
Step Four

Improve your life by choosing
to express more love and less fear.

Express more love to others,
and more love will be expressed to you.

Generate inner peace with your
loving thoughts and experience
a healthier mind and body.

Inhale:
I choose to express love
and experience inner peace.

Exhale:
I release defensive thoughts
and harmful, negative emotions.

Who has not experienced feeling upset or angry at times? When you feel insecure or threatened in some way, it is human tendency to defend yourself in an effort to feel more powerful. You can easily sink into a reactive, negative energy state.

It is important to realize that when you release your sense of fear and self-doubt, you can meet any perceived threats in your life with the supreme force of peace and love. Look to your Soul to awaken your true power. The ability to remain calm, peaceful, and loving in the face of chaos, anger, and tension is beyond powerful.

Truthfully, a disruption to your inner peace is physically costly. Your body suffers when you cave into fear and chaos. In any life situation, you have the option to engage peacefully, or to lovingly disengage: you are wise to disengage if you are losing your ability to remain peaceful and calm.

The numerous benefits of maintaining a calm nervous system include keeping your immune system functioning at its' best and maintaining a balanced (less stressed) cardiovascular system that will remain healthier for a longer period of time. You reduce your risk of disease in all organ systems when you engage life with a peaceful and relaxed mind.

The Love of a Dog Heals the Heart and Soul

Marco had spent 44 years of his life defending himself from perceived threats. In so doing, he had become what he despised in others— a world class bully. He knew inside he felt small and afraid; yet, he was never going to admit that to anyone. So, Marco lived his life in a reactive state of defensiveness and fear.

Marco placed all of his attention on his career in an effort to feel powerful; yet, what he gained in power and status was at the expense of love and relationships. His wife walked away with their infant son 20 years ago. He never fostered a relationship with his now adult son. In fact, his son wanted nothing to do with him, and Marco couldn't really fault him.

During a tense business deal, Marco felt his heart rate escalate. In a fit of rage, he collapsed. He awoke in a hospital frightened, alone, and wishing he would have died.

Marco's medical team looked forward to his discharge from the hospital for he was an extremely angry man, and difficult to interact with. His nurse felt heavy hearted for him. All of her attempts to be kind were met with resistance; so, she called in the master of resistance reduction–Miss Kaile.

Kaile, one of the hospital's therapy dogs, was well known for her ability to melt hardened, lonely hearts. Few patients could resist her sweet, loving, angelic eyes. Kaile was a master at providing pure, healing love to frightened and resistant patients. Marco's nurse decided to make one last attempt to reach the heart of her patient. She opened the door and allowed Kaile to perform her magic.

As she peeked in the room, Marco's nurse witnessed the healing power of love. Kaile's warm presence was all it took. Marco's eyes filled with tears in the presence of Kaile. With joy in her heart, his nurse walked into the room.

Marco gently questioned why a hospital allowed dogs to visit patients. "Because dogs are the greatest healers for sad, lonely, defensive hearts", she replied, while handing him a tissue. She could hear the softness in his voice for the first time since his admission to the hospital.

Marco recounted fond memories of his first dog when he was a young boy. He shared how happy he was remembering the joyful, easy going child he had been before becoming a tense, defensive adult. "I can't believe I allowed myself to become such a defensive bully", he admitted aloud. "Can I speak with Kaile's trainer?" he inquired.

Kaile's trainer gladly met with Marco. Marco expressed his sincere gratitude for Kaile's angelic visit: "It is as if a part of me that was closed down opened up once again. I remembered the non-defensive, loving part of me that got swallowed up years ago. I want to remember love, and feel less defensive."

Marco asked if the trainer knew anyone who might have a therapy dog he could adopt and take to work with him. He knew a dog like Kaile would help him remember unconditional love, even in the most stressful of situations. The trainer joyfully replied, "Well, the lovely Miss Kaile has graduated her dog-therapy training program. Would you like to apply to adopt her?"

Marco could not believe his ears. The very dog that had helped to heal his hardened heart could now be his companion. With a new found liveliness in his soul, he completed the adoption application.

Marco's nurse was thrilled. To her surprise, Marco's son had come to drive his Dad home. Her patient was leaving the hospital with a truly healed heart. The love of a dog had made all the difference. While medicine helped to heal her patient's physical heart; it was LOVE that healed his emotionally wounded heart. Miraculously, her patient had been restored to wholeness.

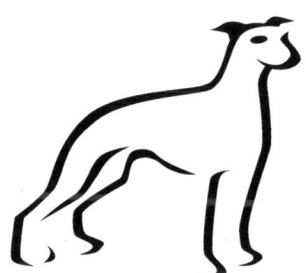

(This story is dedicated to some of the greatest teachers of love I have ever known: Miss Kaile, Tonka, Mica and Halley. What fun times we shared; you are forever in my heart!)

 Relax Your Mind
Mental Exercise

How would you complete the following sentences?

The situation(s) I desire to gain a healthier perspective of, and feel less defensive about is (are):_____.

I choose to accept and love myself so that I can feel at peace about_____.

When you catch yourself feeling defensive about a situation, pause. Be aware of the defensiveness in your heart and accept that it is human tendency to initially react in a fearful way. Now, allow yourself to entertain a healthier perspective. Love, in the highest sense, allows you to see beyond the perceived limits of any challenging situation.

Observe the fearful defensive thoughts in your mind, and in the mind of others. First, love and accept yourself; then, extend that love and acceptance to others. Feel your mind relax as you immerse yourself in a gentle, protective field of love.

Reflections:

When the power of love
overcomes the love of power,
the world will know peace."
—Jimi Hendrix

Relax Your Mind
Step Five

Choose to speak words of love that inspire, encourage, and uplift yourself and others.

Allow your words to honor the goodness of life.

Replace any negative self-talk with words of self-respect and validation.

Inhale:
I speak words that serve a greater good;
my words serve love.

Exhale:
I let go of negative self-talk
and words that serve fear.

The words we speak reflect our soul to the world. Loving souls speak words of kindness, compassion, appreciation, and gratitude. Frightened souls speak words of disrespect, selfishness, competition, and control. Know that every word you speak has a powerful impact on others: your listeners are either uplifted or disheartened by your words.

Your life will seem much easier when you learn to filter unkind words from others: understand that unkind words are a reflection of the speaker's soul. Practice filtering the negative impact of words spoken by a fearful soul, while maintaining your unyielding state of inner peace.

When we meditate and pray, we improve our awareness of the impact of our words on others. We recognize the importance of speaking in a manner that serves to uplift ourselves and others. We release any desire to speak in a self-serving, controlling, or manipulative ways. Allowing a higher consciousness to direct our speech is the most loving choice we can make for humanity.

Honor life with your verbal power. Pay little attention to words spoken that are not supportive, nor encouraging. Know that you have the power to change your world with the words you choose to speak.

Words Serve a Greater Good

Millie clocked in at the grocery store and made her way to the check-out counter. She started her work day as she always did, with a silent prayer that she would be truly helpful to others. She was loved by her co-workers who often left notes of appreciation in her inbox. Frequently she was told how much her encouraging words made a difference in her co-workers' ability to cope with their busy, stressful lives.

Millie enjoyed her job, yet wished she could have attended college and trained to be a social worker. She encountered many people each day that she wanted to help. She resolved to help others as best she could with a kind-hearted interaction as they checked out at the grocery store.

Millie learned the hard way the importance kind words could have upon a weary soul. She grew up with alcoholic parents who never spoke kindly to one another, often yelling insults to one another for hours. They rarely spoke to Millie unless she behaved in a manner that did not please them. Then, the angry words would readily spew forth.

Growing up, Millie's aunt provided her only solace. Her Aunt Fran was such a peaceful lady who spoke words of love and encouragement. Millie spent every Sunday with her aunt and always felt uplifted after these weekly visits. Her Aunt Fran reminded her she would be an adult soon, and she could choose a better life than that led by her parents.

Like her Aunt Fran, Millie chose to

speak words of love and kindness to all she met. She knew that many people had life experiences similar to her own. She was aware that a kind word or a simple smile could make a significant difference in someone's life.

Each evening, Millie would select a daily inspirational quote and print it onto tiny slips of paper. Her customers looked forward to checking out and receiving an inspirational quote for the day. Often she would say a silent prayer for customers who appeared unusually stressed or discouraged. She made it a point to make eye contact and kindly smile at every customer.

Before leaving work one evening, Millie was called into her supervisor's office. She was handed a letter from a long standing customer, Mr. Fee. Millie recalled how burdened he always seemed, and how grateful he was when she handed him an inspirational quote. She opened the letter, and it read:

Dear Millie,

For years, I have been a customer at this store. I would always choose your register because you had a way of brightening my day. Your smile, the inspirational quotes, and your wishes for a pleasant day were music to my weary soul.

My daughter (who is about your age) died six months ago after a courageous effort coping with cancer. You had no way of knowing how distraught I was. I was just another customer in your check-out line. I want to thank you for your reassuring smile and encouraging words.

I am establishing a foundation in memory of my daughter and I need a director. I would truly love to speak with you. I know you exude an angelic, comforting presence. I would be pleased if you would choose to help lead this heart-felt project.

I hope to speak with you soon. I have included my business card and do hope you will call me.

Sincerely,
Mr. Fee

As this story illustrates, you can make a real difference in someone's life with kind words and a smile. You never know the pain in another person's heart. You have the opportunity to serve humanity in a loving way with the words you speak, and the attitude your words reflect to the world.

Humanity is in need of more spiritually aware people who choose to speak of love in the face of doubt and fear. Never forget the power of your loving words spoken to a weary soul. You will enjoy a more gratifying life the more loving you choose to be. As you speak more of love and less of fear, feel your mind relax!

"Watch your manner of speech if you wish to develop a peaceful state of mind. Start each day by affirming, peaceful, contented, and happy attitudes and your days will tend to be pleasant and successful."

—Norman Vincent Peale

Relax Your Mind
Mental Exercise

How would you complete the following sentences?

Situations that I find myself or others speaking negatively and/or fearfully about include _____.

I see the potential to speak more positively and lovingly about the following situations _____.

As you redirect your mind to thoughts of safety, security, and gratitude you become more creative in your approach to life. You begin to trust your inner wisdom and guidance. You steer away from fear-based thinking habits and turn towards more love-based patterns of thought. Your words reflect a state of inner peace, and your life becomes an example for others desiring to increase their sense of inner peace.

Reflections:

"Too often we underestimate the power of a touch, a smile, a kind word, a listening ear, an honest compliment, or the smallest act of caring, all of which have the potential to turn a life around."
~Leo Buscaglia

Relax Your Mind
Step Six

Foster loving thoughts and
improve your life in every way.

Spend more of your mental energy
focused on solutions and less mental
energy focused on problems.

Increase your life-force with loving,
solution-focused thoughts.

Inhale:

I enjoy loving, creative thoughts;
I feel my energy expand into
the infinite field of love.

Exhale:

I release fearful, tense thoughts
that leave me feeling overwhelmed,
and my life-force depleted.

Your mind is very powerful. It is constantly generating thoughts of love, or thoughts of fear. You have a choice to redirect your mind away from fearful, problem-focused thinking toward loving, solution-focused thinking. In so doing, you will live a more relaxed, harmonious, and satisfying life.

Within your inner being are two possible directors of your life story:

(1) Your instinctive problem-focused mind will produce a tale of impossibility and fear.

2) Your inner wisdom will produce a mental tale of infinite possibility and love.

It is your life, and you get to choose your director: your choice will determine the essence and quality of your life story.

Each and every day you are writing the story of your life. Write a story that features you as the courageous hero who learned from challenges and lived a satisfying life. Enjoy the increased life force you feel when you surrender your fear-based mind to your inner wisdom.

Your inner wisdom is waiting to guide you to a more relaxed and peaceful life. You can choose to quiet your fear-based mind and allow your higher self to lead the way. In so doing, at life's end, you will be able to say, "I surrendered my mind to my inner wisdom and created a loving, peaceful, and gratifying life story!" Feel your mind relax as you surrender!

<u>Thoughts of Love Will See You Through!</u>

I came to know Aron Ralston as a fun-loving, enthusiastic music fan. His radiant energy stood out in a crowd. It was always a joy to see his smiling face at a String Cheese Incident or Keller Williams concert.

I was shocked when I saw a photo of Aron on the evening news. The headline stated: Climber Forced to Amputate His Own Arm Survives. My heart sank. I lit a candle and began to pray for Aron and his family. Thoughts of his horrendous experience were too painful for me to consider.

In his book, *127 Hours: Between a Rock and a Hard Place*, Ralston writes in detail about his experience.[4] It was April of 2003, when he headed out alone for a day hike in a remote canyon in the southwest. Upon descending into a narrow slot canyon, an 800 pound boulder suddenly dislodged from above him. In an instant, the boulder crushed his right arm and pinned him to the canyon wall. He was now trapped and alone in this isolated, dark slot canyon.

I was honored to speak with Aron about his experience. This conversation left a lasting impression on my heart. The story he shared with me is a testament to the life-sustaining force we derive when we focus our thoughts on love.

For four days, Aron desperately attempted to free himself by chipping at the rock with his pocket knife. Each day, his hopes for being rescued, or for freeing himself diminished.

On day five, Aron concluded death was certain if he did not proceed to do the unthinkable, amputate his own arm. All he had was his now, quite dull pocket knife. How did he manage to do this life saving, incomprehensible act?

Aron explained he could sense the love of those who were praying most for his safe return— the love of his mother, his father, his sister and his best friend. He stressed to me that it was love that gave him the inner strength needed to do what it took for his survival. He was determined to move beyond his overwhelming fears so that he could be with those he loved once again.

With courage, he surrendered his

fearful mind to his inner wisdom. He made it clear that it was **only love** that elevated him above his mental blocks and fear of death. Love provided him the courage to do what he had to do.

After five unthinkable days, Aron was reunited with his loved ones. I can only imagine the joy of that moment! Love had seen him through!

Aron's experience inspires us to embrace the power of loving thoughts to overcome fearful thoughts: what an inspirational, true story demonstrating the remarkable power of love. I have heard him say, "Love kept me going; love gave me the courage to take one more step."

When we face challenges in our lives, how important it is to turn our thoughts away from fear and toward love. Aron Ralston's story is a reminder that love will lead us to life-enhancing possibilities and away from life-draining impossibilities. For Aron, thinking of love, not fear, was a matter of life and death. How much easier is it for you and I to surrender to love in less critical life situations? I am grateful to him for this powerful message to choose love, not fear.

"Life is about the people I love
and the people who love me...
life is about who you are
and how you love."
—Aron Ralston

Relax Your Mind
Mental Exercise

How would you complete the following sentences?

I tend to become more fearful and problem-focused in the following situation(s) _____.

I choose to focus on a loving solution to the following situation(s): _____.

If you find yourself stuck in a fearful, life-draining situation, think of Aron Ralston. His life is a shining example of the power of love to overcome fear, even the fear of death. There is no situation where a loving solution is not possible. Release your mind from the grips of fear. Go within, focus on the people and/or the things that you love, and feel your mind relax.

Reflections:

"You are today where your thoughts have brought you; you will be tomorrow where your thoughts take you."
—James Allen

Relax Your Mind
Step Seven

Embrace the oneness of all things.

Appreciate that the capacity for life
and for love is a miracle.

Recognize that all of life is sustained
by a common miraculous Source.

Feel the wonder of life;
sense the common ground you
share with all the expressions of life.

Inhale:
The Source of life is within me. I am immersed in the majestic Source of life.

Exhale:
I release thoughts of separation and disharmony.

Reflect upon a time when you were fully enamored by the moment: such as walking on a beach at sunset, hiking in a forest or listening to a soul stirring song. Recall the stillness of that moment, as you experienced all-encompassing gratitude and joy. You no longer had worries or deadlines occupying your mind. You no longer sensed any pain or discomfort in your body. You were in a state of wonder; you were simply "being at one" with that enchanting moment.

Observe your busy, tense mind... running "to-do lists", preoccupied with future worries and fears, dwelling on past regrets. Consider how distracted your mind can be from the present moment, as you focus on tasks yet to be completed. Notice how needy and unsettled your body can be ...hungry, thirsty, tired, sleepy, hot, cold...constantly commanding your attention.

Know that you are capable of experiencing life beyond the mind and body when you allow your soul to embrace the many pleasant moments in your daily life. Allow your soul to bring balance and harmony to your mind and body; enjoy the resulting inner peace.

If you wish to relax your mind, then you must choose to create moments of stillness. Each day of your life, pause and look beyond your mind and body: let your soul guide you to that sweet still space of "Oneness with Life."

Looking Into Infinity

I cradled 74 year old Miss Diana in my arms as though she were a young child in need of comfort. Her energy was soft and peaceful. She giggled and said to me, "My body just can't keep up with my soul any longer; but, I don't feel ready to tip-toe with the angels to the other side just yet." We both knew her body was terminal from cancer, but her spirit had a few topics left to cover with me.

Quietly time passed, as we stared into the mysterious space beyond her life in a human body. Minutes passed in silence; no words needed as love flowed between our hearts. We looked deeply into one another's eyes. I sensed we were truly one. There was no superficial emotional space between us: we were soul to soul.

I experienced a deep inner-knowing that death was nothing to fear. Miss Diana and I would never be separated, as love is not diminished by the death of one's body. I smiled inside, grateful for this inner wisdom and for the peace it brought to my soul. The words she spoke between those silent moments were profound.

Following, are topics she chose to address as she prepared to "tip-toe" out of her body:

Time:

"For some reason, time seems very funny to me", she laughingly commented, "but I still want to know what time it is." I told her the date and time, and we both burst out laughing. We concluded how silly it is to divide your life into hours, days, and months; for in the end, minutes on the clock add up to just one lifetime.

She reminded me, "You know you will die some day; but, when it is your time, you simply can't imagine your life has been lived, and will be ending soon." We contemplated the hours people waste worrying about inconsequential matters. She wished more people could understand "how precious each day truly is in the end" and how important it is to "feel at one with life" each and every day.

"It seems silly how worried I could be about small details sometimes. I am so glad I valued my time with my family and my friends, that is the most important time of all," she stated. I promised her I would remind others to live and love one day at a time, to see how much we have in common with each other, and to realize that hours and days really add up to just one remarkably brief lifetime.

Laughter:

"I so enjoyed all the giggles with my mom, my grandmother, and my friend-Brian" she shared. "Even though I am dying, I still just want to get up and go have some fun. I want to giggle some more, giggles are the best. Wouldn't it be fun if you took me to the mall in this dying body and I purchased a watch right now?" she joked.

We reflected on the lack of separation we felt when sharing laughter with others. As Victor Borge once said, "Laughter is the shortest distance between two people." She thanked me for helping her to laugh today, for not being solemn and despairing as most of her visitors lately. I promised her I would laugh often and take life much less seriously!

Love:

Miss Diana turned to me and said, "You know, I would be glad to have cancer again if it meant I would get to be with you, my dogs, and the people I love again. I want you to know I really love you." We spent some time looking through her scrapbook. I was clearly aware that all the simple moments were what mattered most to her in these final hours.

Her face lit up as she held homemade cards from her boys when they were little. "It really is the simple things that truly matter" she whispered to herself. "I only wish I could have been more loving to everyone I knew, not just to my own family and closest friends. I see now that we are all kindred souls."

She asked me to look beyond external appearances and see the hearts of all the people that I interact with each day. I promised her I would do my very best to spread love to all, and to embrace my life more fully. In a soft angelic voice I heard her say, "We are one, all is one."

I kissed her cheek and tucked her into bed. As I left the room, I knew I would not see her alive again; yet, I felt soothing inner peace from her last words-

<u>"We are one; all is one."</u>

"No man is an island, entire of itself;
every man is a piece of the continent."
—John Donne

Relax Your Mind
Mental Exercise

How would you complete the following sentences?

If I knew this was one of my last days on Earth, I would _____.

I know I take these people/places/things for granted: _____.

I feel most connected to others and to life when _____.

I would like to enjoy a more light-hearted view about _____.

I choose to be more loving toward _____.

I am honored to revisit Miss Diana's words of wisdom, as follows:

- Time is an illusion. Life comes to an end quicker than you could ever imagine. Appreciate each day as if it were going to be your last.

- Love others with all of your heart; the love you choose to share is what matters most in the end.

- Be light-hearted on your journey; see the joy and humor in life. Trade in the days of your life for time spent laughing, and sharing love with others.

- Death does not diminish a lifetime of laughing and loving, as loving hearts are always connected in a mysterious way.

- Appreciate your mind and body, but live from your heart. In the end, matters of the heart are what give life true value.

- At the close of our life, we will truly understand the "oneness" of it all: one lifetime to give love to others, to laugh with others, and to embrace all of the expressions of life.

Reflections:

"There are four questions of value in life: What is sacred? Of what is spirit made? What is worth living for, and what is worth dying for? The answer to each is the same.
Only love."

–Don Juan DeMarco

AFTERWORD

"There has never been a time on Earth like we see today. What we need are more ways to experience our interconnectedness— it is a precursor to deep love.

So in this quickening light, with the dawn of each new day, let us look for love. Let us no longer struggle.

Let us ever become who we most want to be. As we begin to be who we truly are, the world will be a better place."

—John Denver

Dear Reader,

Thank you for reading this book; please know how grateful I am to have shared these words with you.

Each and every day we have the option to open our minds, hearts, and souls to the life-enhancing force of Love. When we choose to move beyond our fear-based minds and fill our minds with thoughts of gratitude, life becomes like a peaceful, majestic dream. When we allow the news media, or talk of political division and economic ruin to fill our minds, life becomes heavy and burdensome like an unpleasant, disturbing dream.

In our information overloaded world, I know we all need to remember the bigger picture of life. Life is about sharing your wisdom and joy with others as you open your heart to the experience of a Higher Power expressed as love. The stories of Viktor Frankl and Aron Ralston as shared in this book so profoundly demonstrate the remarkable power of love. Certainly, love can lead us to inner peace, regardless of external circumstances.

As I learned from Miss Diana, life is precious and brief. Each day of life is a gift. Each day we are given the opportunity to develop healthy self-love, as well as love for all. With love we have much to appreciate, as we experience gratitude for family and friends, sunshine and rain, flowers and tress, birds and wildlife, our pets- the list goes endlessly on. Inner peace awaits you when you embrace life with a loving heart.

I wish for you to experience a relaxed mind and a peaceful life. I hold you, and all of humanity, in my heart with Love!

Elizabeth Jenkins Caspian, M.D.

"It is only when we silent the blaring sounds of our daily existence that we can finally hear the whispers of truth that life reveals to us, as it stands knocking on the doorsteps of our hearts."

−K.T. Jong

Meditation to Relax Your Mind

I am safe and secure. I am grateful
for all that I have.

I am creative and unique; there are
infinite possibilities for my life.

I listen for inner wisdom and trust it to
direct me to my highest truth.

I choose to express love and
experience inner peace.

I speak words that serve a greater good,
my words serve love.

I enjoy loving, creative thoughts;
my energy expands into the
infinite field of love.

I am in awe of the Source of life.
In stillness, I sense my connection to
all the expressions of life.

APPENDIX

The Biopsychosocial Model

First presented by George Engel, MD in 1977, the Biopsychosocial Model is an inclusive theory for understanding health from a holistic point of view. This model points to three domains of human experience that determine one's health status at a given point in time- biological, psychological and social.

The Biopsychosocial Model is a helpful guide for your healing journey. As you will see, there are many variables to consider when you are seeking to reestablish inner peace and a relaxed state of mind. It is wise to follow a multi-modal treatment approach to restoring and maintaining an optimal state of mental and physical health.

On the following pages are the key questions addressed in a Biopsychosocial Assessment. Consider your answers to the questions that follow. You deserve to enjoy optimal mental and physical health; the result of caring for your Biopsychosocial needs and creating positive changes in your life.

"Good for the body is
the work of the body,
good for the soul
the work of the soul,
and good for either
the work of the other."

—Henry David Thoreau

Key Components of a Biopsychosocial Assessment

Social Components:

- Are your basic needs for food, clothing, and housing met at this time?
- Do you have supportive friends and/or family?
- Are your religious beliefs, family structure and culture in harmony with your personal value system?
- Do you feel as if you "belong" to a social group?
- Do you have the mental and physical ability to take care of yourself?
- Do you have healthy hobbies and interests that you enjoy?

Psychological Components:

- Did you have healthy role models as a child?
- Do you have healthy self-respect and respect for others?
- Do you engage in healthy self-soothing habits, such as hiking, reading, or listening to music; habits that bring you back to inner peace when facing challenges in your life?
- Are you able to redirect your mind from problem-focused thinking to solution-focused thinking?
- Are you engaged in activities that promote self improvement and positive coping skills, such as community events, spiritual meetings, inspirational retreats, or working with a healing professional?
- Are you able to see the "bigger picture" of your life?

- Do you see yourself as a valuable member of society?
- Are you willing to self-reflect and make improvements in areas of your life that cause you emotional or physical pain?

Biological Components:

- Are you eating healthy foods?
- Do you exercise regularly?
- Are you getting adequate rest and relaxation time?
- Do you see a doctor/healing professional for routine health check-ups?
- Are you proactive about maintaining your physical health?

Suggested Healthy Brain Habits

Healthy brain habits significantly improve your quality of life. You deserve a balanced life made possible by healthy brain habits.

Social Habits

Surround yourself with positive role models and avoid negative people (including the news media and divisive politicians).

Participate in volunteer projects that benefit others in your community.

Reduce unhealthy, stressful life situations and activities as much as possible; increase healthy relaxing life situations and activities as much as possible.

Psychological Habits

Develop positive, solution-focused thinking skills; seek professional assistance when you feel stuck in negative, problem-focused thinking.

Balance the details of life with the "bigger picture" of life by connecting to nature and a spiritual practice/religious tradition.

Be more present-focused. Avoid dwelling on thoughts of the past or the future. Practice taking life one day at a time.

Biological Habits

Eat healthy food/avoid unhealthy food.

Avoid nicotine, addictive street drugs, and excessive alcohol consumption.

Exercise routinely and gently improve your fitness level.

Get adequate rest and relaxation.

Be proactive about maintaining your physical health.

Consult with respectful, compassionate healing professionals when needed.

ENDNOTES

1. Frankl, Viktor E. <u>Man's Search for Meaning</u>. Boston: Beacon Press, 2006. p. 47.
2. Frankl, Viktor E. p. 36.
3. Frankl, Viktor E. p. 40.
4. Ralston, Aron. <u>127 Hours: Between a Rock and a Hard Place.</u> New York: Atria Paperback, 2004.

"The good physician treats the disease;
the great physician treats the patient
who has the disease."
—William Osler, MD

Dr. Caspian is available for speaking engagements, and for hosting retreats.

Contact information:

Center for Creative Change, LLC
2380 N. Oakmont Drive
Flagstaff, AZ 86004

relaxyourmind123@aol.com

http://relaxyourmind.org

Dr. Elizabeth Caspian invites you to a weekend retreat dedicated to supporting you as you learn to "Relax Your Mind" and create a more gratifying and relaxed life.

Relax Your Mind Training

Dr. Elizabeth Caspian is a passionate teacher of relaxation skills for optimal mental health.

(http://relaxyourmind.org)

She is joined by Teresa Donahue, PTA, PYT- Professional yoga therapist

(www.3byoga.vpweb.com)

and George Denslow, author and life coach

(www.georgedenslow.com).

It is our intention to create a day of learning and relaxing together!

We look forward to supporting your journey to a more relaxed way of life.

For details regarding upcoming retreats, email us at:

relaxyourmind123@aol.com